Finding Temple Symbols

Written by Cami Evans • Illustrated by Jennifer Tolman

CFI • An imprint of Cedar Fort, Inc.
Springville, Utah

Lucy loves to visit the many temples and can hardly wait for the day she can go inside.

As she prepares to enter, Lucy likes to find meaning in the things around her on temple grounds.

There are temples with symbols all over the world. What things can you find outside the different temples?

Can you find the flowers
at the temple?

Beautiful gardens of flowers and plants
are like the many living things God
created for Adam and Eve. Flowers are
a symbol of life and creation.

Can you find the spires
pointing upward from the temple?

The temple spires lift your eyes to
the skies like prayer turns your
thoughts to God in heaven.
Spires are a symbol of looking up to God.

Can you find the angel statue on top of the temple?

The golden angel blows a horn that seems to call out the good news of the gospel like the angels will trumpet the return of Christ at His Second Coming.

The angel Moroni is a symbol of gathering
the righteous for the coming of the Lord.

Can you find the squares on the temple walls?

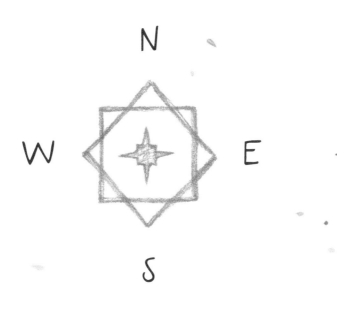

A square has four corners like the earth has four main directions. Squares are a symbol of aligning God's creations from all over the earth.

Can you find
the circles

carved into the temple stones?

A circle has no beginning and no end
like eternity goes on forever.
In the temple, families are sealed together.
Circles are a symbol of heaven and eternity.

Can you find a square and circle together on the temple?

Sometimes symbols are combined for an even greater meaning. A squared circle is a symbol of temples being where earth and heaven meet.

Can you find the
big trees by the temple?

When you live the gospel, the word
of God grows in your heart like a
tiny seed becomes a tree over time.
Trees are a symbol of growing
strong in the gospel.

Can you find
the sun, moon,
and stars on the
temple walls?

If the telestial
kingdom is like the
stars in the sky,
then the terrestrial
kingdom is like the
brighter moon,
and the celestial
kingdom is as
bright as the sun.

The stars, moon, and
sun are symbols of the
three degrees of glory.

Can you find the people wearing white clothes at the temple?

White is clean and bright, which shows that our lives can be spotless as we come unto Christ.

White clothing is
a symbol of being
pure inside.

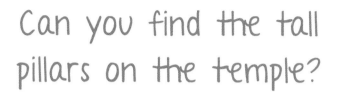

Can you find the tall
pillars on the temple?

Pillars give support to buildings just
like God gives you spiritual strength.
Pillars are a symbol of Heavenly
Father's presence and strength.

Can you find the gate around the temple?

To get to the temple, you must first walk through the gate just like you must be baptized, receive the gift of the Holy Ghost, and live the gospel before receiving your temple blessings.

The temple gate is
a symbol of starting
on the covenant
path that returns to
Heavenly Father.

Can you find water in the temple fountain?

Clean water washes away dirty things and keeps us healthy like Jesus washes away our mistakes and helps our spirits thrive. Water is a symbol of Jesus as the Living Water.

Can you see how the temple glows with light?

Light shining from the temple at night is like sharing the light within you when the world seems dark. The temple is a symbol of our commitment to Jesus, the Light of the World.

Lucy feels peaceful and happy as she finds symbols at the temple. Lucy knows Heavenly Father is preparing her to go inside someday.

If the flowers testify of God's creations, the spires point our eyes and minds to heaven, and the symbols in stones teach of the gospel, what other symbols will you find?

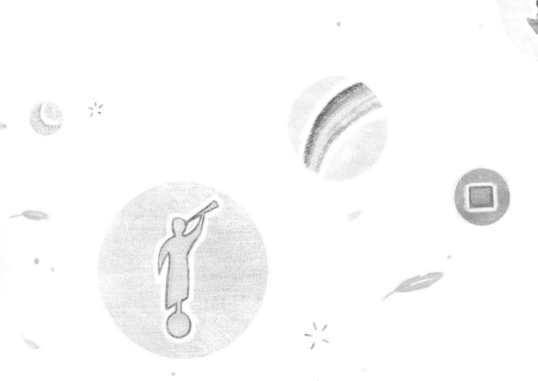

For Sydney, Kenzie, and Lily.
Badaladalada. Life is good! And also for my
great-great-great-great aunt Rosannah.
—Cami

For my sweet boys
Carter, Brigham, and Tommy
—Jennifer

Text © 2019 Cami Evans
Illustrations © 2019 Jennifer Tolman
All rights reserved.

ISBN 13: 978-1-4621-2315-5

Published by CFI, an imprint of Cedar Fort, Inc.
2373 W. 700 S., Springville, UT 84663
Distributed by Cedar Fort, Inc., www.cedarfort.com

Library of Congress Control Number: 2018962537

Cover design and typesetting by Shawnda T. Craig
Cover design © 2019 Cedar Fort, Inc.
Edited by Kaitlin Barwick

Printed in the United States of America

10 9 8 7 6 5 4 3 2 1

Printed on acid-free paper